OUR BODY

Muscular System

Cheryl Jakab

MACMILLAN
LIBRARY

First published in 2006 by
MACMILLAN EDUCATION AUSTRALIA PTY LTD
627 Chapel Street, South Yarra 3141

Visit our website at www.macmillan.com.au

Associated companies and representatives throughout the world.

National Library of Australia
Cataloguing-in-Publication data

Jakab, Cheryl.
   Muscular system.

   Includes index.
   For upper primary aged children.
   ISBN 978 0 7329 9866 0.
   ISBN 0 7329 9866 2.

   1. Muscles – Juvenile literature. I. Title.
   (Series: Jakab, Cheryl. Our body).

612.74

Edited by Ruth Jelley
Text and cover design by Peter Shaw
Illustrations by Guy Holt, Jeff Lang (p. 4 (bottom), pp. 5–6),
   and Ann Likhovetsky (p. 30)
Photo research by Legend Images

Printed in China

Acknowledgements
The author and the publisher are grateful to the following for permission to reproduce
copyright material:

Front cover photograph: Coloured SEM/scanning electron micrograph of
freeze-fractured skeletal muscle fibre, courtesy of Photolibrary/Steve Gschmeissner/
Science Photo Library.
Front cover illustration by Jeff Lang.

Sercomi-B.S.I.P./Auscape International, p. 16; Bill Thomas/Imagen, p. 28; Photodisc,
pp. 18, 19, 21, 22, 23; Photolibrary/Science Photo Library, pp. 9, 10, 17, 26.

While every care has been taken to trace and acknowledge copyright, the publisher tenders
their apologies for any accidental infringement where copyright has proved untraceable.
Where the attempt has been unsuccessful, the publisher welcomes information that would
redress the situation.

Contents

Body systems

Amazing body structures   4
The muscular system   5

Anatomy
Structure

Parts of the muscular system   6

Physiology
How the muscular system works

Contraction   14

Paediatrics and nutrition
Growth and development

Controlling movement   18
Healthy muscles   22

Pathology and diagnosis
Diseases and treatment

Muscular problems   24
Treating problems   26

You and your muscular system

Taking care of the muscular system   28
Make a model arm **ACTIVITY**   30
Glossary   31
Index   32

Glossary words
When a word is printed in **bold**,
you can look up its meaning
in the Glossary on page 31.

Amazing body structures

The human body is an amazing living thing. The structures of the body are divided into systems. Each system is made up of **cells**. Huge numbers of cells make up the **tissues** of the body systems. Each system performs a different, vital function. This series looks at six of the systems in the most familiar living thing to you – your body.

Cells make up tissues of the body systems.

circulatory system   digestive system   muscular system

The muscular system

The muscular system moves all of your body parts. How much do you know about your muscular system?

- How many muscles do you have?
- What does each muscle do in your body?
- How do your muscles change as you grow?
- What happens if you tear a muscle?

This book looks at the human muscular system to answer these questions and more.

nervous system

respiratory system

skeletal system

Parts of the muscular system

The muscular system is made up of all the **skeletal muscles** in the body. Skeletal muscles are voluntary muscles, which are controlled by deliberate actions. When we want to move part of our body, a nerve signal is sent from the brain to the muscle, which makes it **contract**.

Other types of muscle in the body, cardiac muscle and smooth muscle, are not part of the muscular system. These muscles are different from skeletal muscles because they are involuntary muscles, which are automatically controlled by the nervous system. They work constantly without you having to think about them. Cardiac and smooth muscles are also made up of different types of **muscle fibre** to skeletal muscles.

! FASCINATING FACT
The muscular system is the largest part of the human body. It makes up about half of the body's total weight.

nasalis
trapezius
zygomaticus major
deltoid
pectoralis major
rectus abdominus
biceps brachii
triceps
quadriceps femoris
tibialis anterior
gastrocnemius

Skeletal muscles are used to move the body.

Skeletal muscles

Skeletal muscles attach to the bones of the skeleton. Most skeletal muscles attach to one bone and stretch across a joint to attach to another bone. There are about 640 muscles that work together to move the various parts of the body.

Superficial and deep muscles

The muscular system is made up of two overlapping layers of muscles, called superficial and deep muscles. Superficial muscles are located on the surface, just under the skin. Deep muscles form a layer beneath the superficial muscles.

TRY THIS

See for yourself

Get a joint of meat, such as a shoulder of lamb, from the butcher. Carefully take the joint apart to see bundles of muscle fibres. Look for the places where the muscles attach to the bones.

deep muscles

superficial muscles

Muscles give the body its shape.

Front and back muscles

The muscles on the front and back of the body have different patterns. The front of the body has three layers of **abdominal** muscles, each running in a different direction. These layers form a strong wall over the stomach area where there are no bones covering internal organs. On the back of the body, the muscles attach to the spine and form a massive triangle.

FASCINATING FACT
The largest muscle in the body is the gluteus maximus in the buttocks, which is involved in leg movements. The smallest muscle in the body, the stapedius, is in the ear. It contracts to protect the ear from very loud sounds.

trapezius

trapezius

serratus anterior

rectus abdominis

external oblique adominal

gluteus maximus

latissimus dorsi

The front muscles (left) help protect internal organs, while the back muscles (right) help hold the spine upright.

Muscle fibres

Muscles are made up of long, string-like fibres which run parallel to each other. They occur in bundles with a covering around them, called a **sheath**. Each fibre is thinner than a human hair and very long. One muscle fibre can be up to 30 centimetres long. Muscle fibres change in length by contracting and relaxing. Contracting shortens muscle fibres. The fibres are at their longest when the muscle is relaxed.

contracted muscle —

— relaxed muscle

Muscle fibres shorten when the muscle contracts.

Skeletal muscle fibres
UNDER THE MICROSCOPE

Skeletal muscle fibres are striped, or striated. This means that they have light and dark bands in the cells.

Tendons

Tendons link muscles to bones. They are strong bands of connecting tissue which form from the ends of the muscle sheath. The end of the tendon passes through the outer covering of bone (the periosteum) to firmly anchor inside the bone.

Tendons can be long or short. Hands have very long tendons which connect the fingers to the muscles in the forearm that control them.

The outer sheath of some tendons, such as in those in the knee, produce a **lubricant**. This lubricant protects the tendons where they rub against bones during movement.

Tendon fibres
UNDER THE MICROSCOPE

Tendon fibres are made of a strong stringy material called collagen. They are much stronger than muscle fibres.

bone

tendon

muscle

tendon

bone

Tendons join the muscle to bone above the knee and in the heel.

peroneus longus

tibialis anterior

gastrocnemius

achilles tendon

The muscles in the lower leg control the movement of the foot.

Leg and foot muscles

Leg and foot muscles work together in activities such as walking, running, cycling and dancing. Strong tendons attach these muscles across the joints of the hip, knee, ankle and toes.

The large, powerful **thigh** muscles surround the largest bone in the body, the femur. These muscles **originate** in the hip and join the femur just above the knee. The calf muscle (gastrocnemius) in the lower leg is smaller than the thigh muscles but still very powerful. The gastrocnemius originates above the knee at the back of the femur and joins the bone at the heel. The muscles in the front of the lower leg have very long tendons which connect to the toes.

FASCINATING FACT
The Achilles tendon attaches the gastrocnemius to the heel. It is named after the Ancient Greek hero, Achilles, whose one weakness was in his heel. In the ancient story, Achilles was killed by an arrow shot into his heel.

The shoulder

The shoulder is controlled by a team of muscles which surround the joint. It is the most **flexible** of all the joints in the body and can be moved in full circles. The deltoid muscle wraps over the shoulder to firmly hold the joint in place.

Arm and hand muscles

The muscles in the hand and lower arm control the hand, giving it a wide range of movement. The muscles of the lower arm are connected to the fingers by very long tendons which run down the forearm to the fingertips. This allows the hands to be small while being very strong. If the forearm muscles themselves were in the hand then the fingers would be very thick. They would be unable to perform fine and precise movements, such as writing.

deltoid

pectoralis major

brachioradialis

Long muscles in the forearm control the tendons in the hand.

thenar muscles

tendons

12

Facial muscles

Facial muscles contract to produce facial expressions such as smiling, frowning, looking sad and laughing. There are about 30 muscles that change the shape of the face. Facial muscles are attached at one end to the skull bones. The other ends of the muscles are attached to the skin, not bones. So when facial muscles contract, they pull the skin into different shapes.

Facial expressions

Each facial expression is made using a range of muscles. Very small changes in the shape of the face can express different feelings. Contracting the zygomaticus muscles, for instance, creates a smile by lifting the corners of the mouth. It is easier to smile than frown because it takes about half as many muscles.

TRY THIS

Flare your nostrils

Try flaring your nostrils wide. You can do this by contracting the levator labii superioris muscles strongly. Practising flaring the nostrils can help strengthen these muscles.

nasalis

frontalis

zygomaticus major

zygomaticus minor

levator labii superioris

There are many muscles in the face which are used to create facial expressions.

Contraction

Contracting a muscle moves the bones or skin the muscle is attached to. For example, contracting the biceps muscle causes the arm to bend at the elbow. Most of the muscles in the body work in this way.

Contraction of the biceps muscle causes the elbow to bend.

Pulling force

When a muscle contracts it applies a pulling force which pulls the bone. The pulling force is applied at the point where the tendon joins the bone. Contracting the biceps muscle pulls the bones in the forearm, the radius and ulna, towads the shoulder. This movement causes the elbow joint to bend. The origin of a muscle stays in a fixed position as the muscle contracts. The origin of the biceps muscle is attached to the shoulder, which remains still as the arm bends.

origin

radius

biceps

tendons

ulna

humerus

Bending and straightening

The biceps muscle contracts to bend the arm, but it cannot push to straighten the arm again. Another muscle, the triceps, must contract to straighten the arm. The biceps muscle relaxes as the triceps muscle contracts, so it does not fight the movement of the arm. When the biceps muscle contracts, the triceps muscle relaxes.

Muscle pairs

The biceps and triceps muscles work as a pair to move the forearm. Any two muscles that work together as a pair are called **antagonists**. Their actions are opposite to each other. When one contracts, the other relaxes. Muscles all over the body work in this way to coordinate all of the body's movements.

biceps contracted

triceps relaxed

The biceps and triceps muscles move the forearm in different directions.

biceps relaxed

triceps contracted

TRY THIS

Find muscle pairs

Find a muscle pair by placing your hands on the front and back of your lower leg. Point your foot down to feel the gastrocnemius contract. Which muscle contracts when you lift your toes back up towards your knee?

How muscles contract

When a muscle gets the signal to contract, each long fibre within the muscle shortens. There are **filaments** within the muscle fibres that slide over each other when a muscle contracts. This makes each fibre shorter so the overall muscle is shorter.

filaments

contracted muscle fibre

filaments

relaxed muscle fibre

Filaments slide over each other to shorten the muscle when it contracts.

Muscle fibre bands UNDER THE MICROSCOPE

There are bands, or striations, within muscle fibres. Contraction occurs within these bands. A microscope shows the striations in the fibres are closer together when a muscle is contracted.

Energy for muscles

Muscles need **energy** to contract. The action of filaments sliding over each other uses up energy and produces **waste**. Muscles use a form of energy called glucose, which is carried to the muscle in the bloodstream. Wastes produced in the muscles are also carried away in the blood. The body creates glucose from the food that is eaten.

Muscle heat and sweat

When muscles work hard they produce heat, which causes the skin to produce sweat. Sweating is the body's way of keeping muscles cool.

A thermogram, or heat picture, shows the amount of heat that is produced by the body. The different colours show that varying amounts of heat are produced in different areas. White indicates areas that are producing the most heat, followed by red, yellow, green, blue and purple. Black areas are those which produce the least amount of heat.

FASCINATING FACT

Oxygen is needed for the muscles to burn glucose. When you exercise, breathing increases in order to deliver the extra oxygen that is needed by the muscles.

A thermogram shows this tennis player is losing the most heat through the abdomen, head, chest and arms.

Controlling movement

Very young babies have little **muscle tone** and cannot control their movements. Skilful movements, such as walking and writing, are developed over many years. Although everybody develops slightly differently, there is a general pattern of muscle development that babies go through.

FASCINATING FACT
Newborn babies automatically grasp objects that are put into their hands. This is known as a reflex action. It is thought that babies develop this reflex to help them hold on to their mothers.

Hand and arm muscles

As hand and arm muscles develop, a child's skill in holding and moving objects increases. At around six months old babies can pass objects from one hand to the other. After about 18 months they can hold a crayon and scribble. By the time they are three years old, control of their hand muscles allows them to copy lines and draw within shapes. By the age of four years, children can copy letters and draw figures. Most five-year-old children can copy shapes and write letters. These precise movements require a great deal of fine control over the muscles in the arms and hands.

Good control of the hand and arm muscles is necessary for writing and drawing.

Developing major muscles

Muscles that are used for sitting, crawling, walking and running develop tone gradually over the first two years of a child's life. Newborn babies do not have strong neck muscles and cannot hold up their heads. At one month old, most babies still lie on their backs with their head to the side. By the age of three years most children can run with ease and kick a ball. This may take longer for some toddlers, while others develop these skills earlier. Skill in moving the body increases with repeated practice. Whether it is playing the piano, tap dancing or kicking a soccer ball, strength and control of muscles is developed through practice. Repetition builds muscle strength and allows actions to be performed without having to think about them.

Strong neck and shoulder muscles are needed to hold up the head and chest.

FASCINATING FACT
Even thinking about practising actions can help improve muscular skills. Many sports coaches find mental rehearsal (going over the actions in the mind) assists in refining motor skills.

Muscles and posture

All the muscles in the **torso** and **limbs** remain partially contracted to maintain **posture**. They must be strong enough to hold the body upright. The powerful muscles of the back hold the spine in the correct position while sitting and standing. These muscles also provide strength for lifting and pushing movements.

Sitting up straight and standing tall help strengthen the smaller deep muscles along the spine. When sitting still or working on the computer for a long time, many muscles are constantly contracted and need a rest. Doing something different, such as standing or walking, will help to rest those muscles.

HEALTH TIP
Exercise

Exercising all the muscles in the body is necessary for overall fitness. Slow, controlled movements using all the different muscles of the body help develop overall muscle tone.

Tip: Exercise programs such as Tai Chi are ideal for developing overall muscle tone.

neck

back

buttocks

thighs

Large muscles in the neck, back, buttocks and thighs are used to hold the body upright.

Muscular differences

Boys and girls have very similar muscular development before **puberty**. As they mature, however, the pattern of muscle development is different in males and females. Adult males generally have broader shoulders with stronger arm and chest muscles than females. Men are stronger in the upper body than women, compared to their overall body size.

FASCINATING FACT
Weight-lifting is an Olympic sport that is designed to test muscle strength. The weight-lifters are classed according to body size, the smallest being the 55 kilogram class. The heaviest weight lifted at the Athens Olympics in 2004 was 267 kilograms.

Males develop stronger muscles than females after puberty.

Healthy muscles

Muscles that are regularly worked hard become strong and healthy. Exercise builds up muscle tissue and makes each fibre stronger. In the past, most people got a great deal of exercise each day which helped keep their muscles healthy. People used to walk everywhere, whereas now we use faster forms of transport, such as cars and trains. Many people today spend much of their time sitting at a desk or a computer for work and entertainment. This sort of lifestyle leads to loss of strength and tone in muscles.

HEALTH TIP
Energy for exercise
Athletes can load up on energy by eating high carbohydrate foods. The energy is stored as a complex sugar known as glycogen, which is converted to glucose when the muscles work.

Tip: Eat high carbohydrate foods two days before a hard workout.

Exercise programs

Exercise programs should give every muscle a workout. Swimming is one type of exercise that involves all the muscles of the body and is gentle on joints. The water also helps cool the muscles as they work.

Swimming helps to build muscle strength by exercising all the muscles in the body.

Maintaining muscle tone

Constant contraction of the back and neck muscles maintains muscle tone. These muscles remain contracted even when we are not moving, in order to hold up the head and keep the spine upright. The brain constantly sends messages to these muscles to keep them contracted. Maintaining good posture helps to keep these muscles strong so that they can hold the body in the correct position.

Flexibility

Muscles and tendons need to be flexible as well as strong. Stretching exercises can help maintain and improve flexibility. This is particularly important for tendons and muscles that are not used very often.

A lacrosse player stretches his legs before a game.

Muscles during sleep

Most muscles relax during sleep, but some of them remain contracted. If you watch somebody fall asleep you can see their muscles slowly relax.

FASCINATING FACT

Gymnasts develop strong arm and hand muscles to hold their whole body weight for doing handstands. Eventually they develop automatic balance in handstands, just as most people do for standing on their feet.

Muscular problems

Muscles do not suffer from many diseases. However, muscle strains or tears can occur during strenuous exercise or in an accident. If one part of a muscle is damaged another part can grow larger and stronger to replace the damaged fibres.

Muscle strain

Damage to muscle fibres is called a muscle strain. This can cause bleeding, soreness, swelling and bruising in the affected muscle. If the damage involves a large number of muscle fibres the injury is called a muscle tear.

Muscular dystrophy

Muscular dystrophy is a set of muscle diseases that cause skeletal muscles to shrink and waste away. Sufferers eventually lose the ability to use their muscles. There is no known treatment, but stretching exercises and surgery can help some sufferers. Scientists continue to research and find out more about the condition.

Poliomyelitis

Poliomyelitis (polio) is a nerve disease that leads to loss of muscle in the affected parts of the body. This disease was once common but was brought under control in the 1940s.

deltoid

tear

humerus

A muscle can tear during exercise, particularly if the body is not properly prepared.

Tendon problems

Tendons, and the sheath around them, can suffer from a number of problems.

Tendonitis

Tendonitis, the swelling of tendons, occurs when tendons rub against bones. Tennis and squash players often experience pain in the shoulder due to the rubbing of the supraspinous tendon on the shoulder blade bone. The swelling increases the rubbing of the tendon, so rest is needed to allow the tendon to return to normal. Walking in poorly fitted shoes can cause the large tendon sheath at the front of the foot to swell.

Tendon tears

A sudden and strong muscle contraction can cause a tendon to tear away from the bone. The extensor tendon on the top of the finger can tear if an object, such as a ball, hits the tip of the finger. Sometimes tendons in the ankle are torn when the ankle is twisted.

FASCINATING FACT
Repetitive Strain Injury (RSI) occurs in people who repeat finger actions continuously, such as piano players and keyboard users. RSI causes swelling of the tendons in the wrist, which leads to severe pain when the fingers are moved.

torn tendon

A torn finger tendon can take several months to heal.

Treating problems

A physiotherapist uses special equipment to help teach a patient to stand and walk.

Physiotherapists treat muscle and tendon problems. Physiotherapy can help with muscle and tendon damage and postural problems.

Relearning to use muscles

After an accident or a long period of bed rest, patients often have to learn how to use their muscles again. Physiotherapy can help people relearn to use their muscles in a way that best suits their needs.

Muscle biopsy

A muscle biopsy, where a small piece of muscle tissue is taken, is sometimes done to diagnose muscle disease. A hollow needle is inserted into the muscle and takes out a core of tissue. This tissue can be examined under a microscope to see if the fibres are normal.

FASCINATING FACT

Muscle biopsy has been used to study muscles in athletes. Scientists have found that sprinters develop more quick-acting fibres while weight-lifters develop more slow-acting fibres.

Surgery

Most tendon tears will heal with rest and physiotherapy treatment. Severely torn tendons need to be rejoined by surgery. A badly torn Achilles tendon is a fairly common sports injury, particularly in tennis players and sprinters who use explosive bursts of muscle contraction.

Stretched tendons

Sometimes tendons become stretched, making muscle contractions ineffective. In extreme cases these tendons need surgery to shorten them.

gastrocnemius

Achilles tendon

tear

A severely torn Achilles tendon must be reattached during surgery.

FASCINATING FACT

Lifting weights was once considered to be an exercise for young men only. More and more elderly people are now doing regular weight-lifting exercises to help keep their muscles toned. Lifting weights is now a very popular form of exercise for the elderly.

Taking care of the muscular system

Healthy muscles work better if they are cared for correctly. This includes being careful when exercising and providing muscles with the energy they need.

Warm up and down

Warming up and down when exercising is one easy way to reduce the risk of damage to muscles. Warm up by moving slowly for a few minutes. Then stretch the muscles that will be under the most strain. Carry out the reverse procedure to warm down after exercising.

A sports teacher shows students how to stretch their thigh muscles before exercise.

Massage

Massage can help keep muscles relaxed, which helps them work better. Massage is the process of rubbing muscles to make sure that they relax fully. Many athletes get regular massages to help recover from strenuous exercise.

HEALTH TIP
Strenuous activities

Strenuous activities that increase muscle strength pull very hard on tendons.

Tip: Use stretches to prevent tendon injuries.

First aid

First aid is important for quick recovery from muscular injuries. If muscles are damaged during physical activity, there is a four-step first aid procedure to follow. This is known as RICE, which stands for Rest, Ice, Compression and Elevation. RICE can aid recovery by reducing swelling and the risk of bruising.

In case of emergency

If you are nearby when someone is severely injured, you should:
- stay calm
- ask the injured person what hurts
- keep the injured person comfortable, but do not move them
- get medical assistance.

Be prepared

It is important to be prepared for emergencies. Learn emergency service numbers and practise what to ask for (police, ambulance or fire services). In Australia, emergency services are contacted by ringing 000. In New Zealand the number to ring is 999.

Rest the injured part immediately and apply ice.

Apply compression (firm pressure), such as a bandage.

Elevate, or raise the injured part.

Make a model arm

You can make a model to show how paired muscles move the arm.

What you need

- 2 rubber bands, cut to lie flat (muscles)
- 2 pieces of string, half the length of the rubber (tendons)
- 2 pieces of cardboard, three times longer than the rubber (bones)
- 1 large split pin
- hole punch
- scissors
- sticky tape

What to do

1 Overlap the two 'bones' and join in the middle with the split pin.

2 Punch holes in the bones, about halfway down on both sides.

3 Tie the pieces of string to one end of both rubber bands.

4 Tie the other end of the string to the hole in one bone. Tie the other end of the rubber to the hole in the other bone. Make sure the rubber bands are tight, but not over-stretched when the 'arm' is straight.

5 Put sticky tape over the holes, to hold the string and rubber firm.

6 Move the bones like an arm bending at the elbow to see how the antagonist muscles work. One band will stretch as the other one loosens.

Glossary

abdominal	in the abdomen, the area below the chest
antagonists	muscles that work opposite each other; one relaxes as the other contracts
cells	the smallest units of living things
contract	shorten
energy	fuel for the body
filaments	very thin strands within muscle fibres that allows muscles to shorten, or contract
flexible	able to bend or move freely
limbs	arms and legs
lubricant	liquid that allows smooth movement by reducing friction
muscle fibre	long strands of muscle tissue
muscle tone	strength in the muscles that hold the body up
originate	start from
posture	the position of the body when sitting, standing or walking
puberty	a stage when young people's bodies mature and become more adult
sheath	coating or covering of a muscle or tendon
skeletal muscles	the muscles that control body movements by moving bones
tendons	strong bands of tissue that connect muscles to bones
thigh	upper leg, above the knee
tissues	groups of similar cells that make up the fabric of body systems
torso	the trunk of the body, from the shoulders down to the buttocks
waste	unwanted products produced by the body

Index

A

abdominal muscles 8
Achilles tendon 11, 27
antagonists 15, 30
arm muscles 10, 12, 14, 15,
    18, 21, 23, 30
athletes 22, 26, 28

B

babies' muscles 18–19
back muscles 8, 20, 23
biceps 6, 14, 15
bones 7, 8, 10, 11, 14

C

calf muscle 6, 11, 15
cardiac muscle 6
cells 4, 9
contraction 6, 9, 14–17, 20, 23

D

deep muscles 7, 20
deltoid 6, 12

E

energy 17, 22
exercise 17, 20, 22, 24, 27, 28

F

facial muscles 13
filaments 16
fingers 10, 12, 25
first aid 29
flexibility 12, 23
foot 11, 15
front muscles 8

G

gastrocnemius 6, 11, 15
gluteus maximus 8

H

hand 10, 12, 18, 23

I

injuries 24, 25, 26, 27, 29
involuntary muscles 6

J

joints 7, 11, 12, 14

L

leg muscles 11, 15, 23

M

massage 28
muscle biopsy 26
muscle fibres 6, 7, 9, 10, 16,
    17, 22, 24, 26
muscle heat 17, 22
muscle pairs 15, 30
muscle shortening 9, 16, 17
muscle tears 5, 24
muscle tone 18, 19, 20, 22,
    23, 27
muscular dystrophy 24

N

neck muscles 19, 23
nerve signals 6, 16

O

origin 14
oxygen 17

P

physiotherapy 26, 27
poliomyelitis 24
posture 20, 23

S

sheath 9, 10, 25
shoulder 7, 12, 14, 19, 21, 25
skeletal muscles 6, 7, 9
smooth muscles 6
strains 24, 25, 28
stretching 23, 24, 28
superficial muscles 7
surgery 24, 27

T

tendons 10, 11, 12, 14, 23,
    24, 25, 26, 27, 28, 30
tendon fibres 10
tendon tears 10, 25, 27
thigh muscles 11, 28
triceps 6, 15

V

voluntary muscles 6

W

warming up 28
weight-lifting 21, 26, 27